Black Book

Java™ 8 Exception Handling

Mahavir DS Rathore

Books by Mahavir DS Rathore

a. Java 8 Exception Handling Quiz
b. Learn Java 8 in a Week

Copyright
Java™ 8 Exception Handling by Mahavir DS Rathore. While every precaution has been taken in the preparation of this book the author assume No responsibility for errors or omissions, or for damages resulting from the use of the information contained herein.

About the author
I have been programming & teaching Java for last 18 years. This book is an effort to document my knowledge to share with everyone across the world. I am available to do training on Java anywhere in the world. My email id is gurumahaveer@gmail.com.

Who should read the book?
This book is for programmers who already know Core Java (Java Standard Edition) and interested to acquire better and deeper understanding of exception handling.

Acknowledgement
Java is owned by Oracle and trademark is acknowledged.

Dedication
To the inventors of the Java Language.

Source Code
For source code of this book please send me a mail at gurumahaveer@gmail.com.

Feedback
Please share your feedback, it will help me in improving the book.

Table of Content

Chapter 1:
Software Setup

Topics
- ✓ **Introduction**
- ✓ **Software Required**
- ✓ **Verifying Installation**
- ✓ **Summary**

Introduction
In this chapter I will show how to download and install the required software needed for learning exception handling using Java. There are many options available to have the required setup based upon operating system.

Java is free to download technology platform from oracle, many languages are supported on Java platform. Wikipedia has an exhaustive list of all JVM languages which can be seen by visiting https://en.wikipedia.org/wiki/List_of_JVM_languages .

Software Required
To develop Java programs you would need at the minimum
- a. Java SE Development Kit 1.8 (Java 8)
- b. Code editor

In this book I will be using Java on Windows OS.

Let's look at various software that are needed and from where we can get them.

a. Java SE Development Kit – http://www.oracle.com/technetwork/java/javase/downloads/ jdk8-downloads-2133151.html

This is Java Standard Edition. Ensure you choose the correct JDK i.e. after identifying operating system and architecture (32 bit or 64 bit). The latest version is 8. It is very important to be cautious when downloading and installing Java, many programmers make a mistake of just downloading JRE and installing it. JRE is the minimum environment required by a Java program to run whereas JDK is the minimum environment to compile and execute Java program, ensure you download JDK not JRE.

b. Code editor – I prefer to use Notepad++. Notepad++ is a great code editor, it has support for over 24 languages and it is open source.The latest version can be download from: https://notepad-plus-plus.org/download/ v6.8.8.html.You can also use other code editors or IDE such as eclipse, netbeans etc.

Verifying Installation

On 32 bit Windows the Java SE is installed in "C:\Program Files (x86)\Java" by default. On 64 bit Windows it is installed in "C:\Program Files\Java" by default.

To check if JDK is installed on your PC go to command line and run
    a. Java Compiler by typing "Javac.exe"
    b. Java Interpreted by typing "java.exe"

If for any of the above command you get a message "is not recognized as an internal or external command" then set the PATH environment variable using control panel. The steps are as follows
    a. Start control panel
    b. Click System applet
    c. Click Advanced system settings
    d. Choose advanced tab
    e. Choose Environment variables button
    f. Set PATH variable to location of javac.exe

Verify the setup by running a "HelloWorld" program.

```
// Program 1
// Description: HelloWorld program
            class Program {
            public static void main(String args[]) {
                System.out.println("Helloworld - Java Exception Handling");
            }
            }
```

Summary
    To develop Java programs a programmer require JDK. JDK can be downloaded from oracle website. To code out Java programs programmer can use a code editor such notepad++.

Chapter 2
What is Exception?

<u>**Topics**</u>
- ✓ **What is an Error?**
- ✓ **Cause of an Exception**
- ✓ **Why to Handle Exception?**
- ✓ **Summary**

What is an Error?
Error is an unexpected situation within a program at compile or runtime. A Java error can occur at compile time or runtime. Let's understand compile time error with the help of an example

```
// Program 1
// Description: Compile time error
class Program {
 public static void Main(String args[]) { // 'M' of Main is upper case - compiler error
    System.out.println("Namaskara Java")  // There is no semi colon - compiler error
 }
}
```

When the above program is compiled, compiler will give compiler errors. This is the first kind of error that Java gives.

The second kind of error is generated when the program is running. This type of error is called an Exception. In other words Exception is an error that occur at runtime. When an Exception occur it will stop the program abruptly. This would be disastrous for mission critical applications such as Banking, Military, Ticketing etc. Hence increasing the reliability of an application is very important and that is why Exception handling is of highest importance.

Let's write a program that would stop (crash) abruptly.

```
// Program 2
// Description : Runtime error i.e Exception
class Program {
 public static void main(String args[]) {
   int i=0;
   int j=10/i; // yields in Arithmetic Exception
 }
}
```

In the above program when the integer is divided by zero program abruptly crashes. We don't want this to happen hence so we perform Exception handling.

Let's look at another program which crashes abruptly.

```
// Program 3
// Description: Runtime Exception – Array out of bounds

class Program {
 public static void main(String args[]) {
  args = new String[1];
  args[0] ="Ram"; // ArrayOutOfBounds exception if no argument is passed
  System.out.println(args[0]);
  }
 }
```

In the above program I show you another instance of an Exception occurence. As we can infer that this program will also crash. When faced with situation like this we perform exception handling.

Causes of an Exception
An Exception may occur in one of the three ways.
   a. The programmer can raise an exception using "throw" keyword. This is mainly done to raise user defined exception.

   b. Abnormal code execution yields into an exception. These exceptions are mainly predefined such as IOException, ArithmeticException, SocketException etc.

   c. When a program is out of memory or the JVM finds byte code is corrupt the application will certainly going to crash. These types of exceptions are called as Asynchronous exception. Programmer cannot handle an asynchronous exception.

Why to Handle Exception?
In a single sentence it can said "software is very pervasive". Today software directly or indirectly impacts many domains such as banking, healthcare, business, military, education, government etc. Hence software reliability if of highest importance and exception handling help to enhance software reliability.

There have been many examples of software crashing the business. Some of the the recent example are

   • Tokyo stock exchange crashes
   • Amazon Christmas Glitch
   • Microsoft Azure Crashes
   • UK border and immigration system

Summary

Error is of two types i.e. compiler and runtime. Exceptions occur at runtime. If an exception is not handled it will crash the program. Exception can occur in one the 3 ways. Exception handling increases the reliability of an application.

Chapter 3
What is Exception Handling?

Topics
- ✓ **What is Exception Handling?**
- ✓ **Need for Exception Handling**
- ✓ **Performing Exception Handling**
- ✓ **Summary**

What is Exception Handling?
Exception handling is the process of responding to runtime error that happen during program execution. It is a mechanism to capture and identify runtime error to avoid abrupt crash of a program. Exception handling helps in avoiding sudden crash of a program, using it programmer can provide a diagnosis of the runtime error. Exception handling changes the flow of the program, using it user can recover exceptional situation in an application. In simple words it is a plan 'B' when something goes wrong within the program at runtime.

Not all runtime errors are recoverable certain exceptions which are called as Asynchronous exceptions cannot be recovered e.g. Out of memory error.

Need for Exception Handling
Using Exception handling programmer can propagate exception on the call stack, which help in identifying the cause of the exception. Java has support for nested exception handling up to any depth. Exception handling is used for identifying and grouping the runtime error which yields in quicker diagnosis. All the above efforts help in improving the reliability and quality of the Java program hence reducing the mean time between failure of an application and this is the prime objective of exception handling i.e. increasing the reliability of a program.

Performing Exception Handling
Exception handling in Java is done with the help of exception handling keywords. There are five keyword that are used for performing exception in java. These keywords are listed below.

a. Try block –   It identifies the code area which encapsulate the vulnerable code.

b. Catch block– It is used for identifying the unique exception which is might occur. Catch block help in grouping providing diagnosis for the occurred exception.

c. Finally block – It used for performing housing keeping jobs.
d. Throw keyword – It is used for raising an exception.

e. Throws keyword – It is used for declaring an exception for a method.

Let's now see a program that uses throw keyword.

```
// Program 1
// Description: How to use 'throw' keyword

class Program {
        public static void main(String args[]) {
                throw new ArithmeticException();
        }
}
```

In above program I demo how to raise an exception using throw keyword.

Summary
Exception handling is principally done to enhance reliability of an application. Exception handing in Java is accomplished using five keywords i.e. try, catch, finally, throw and throws.

Chapter 4
Java Exception Hierarchy

Exception Hierarchy

Java has specific class hierarchy within its API which accommodates the Exception classes. The Throwable class is the mother class of all exception classes in Java. Below is schematic diagram that represents Java exception hierarchy.

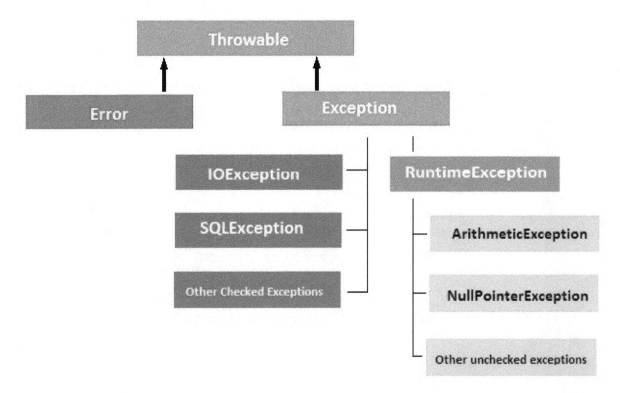

Basically there are four classes that are of vital importance i.e Throwable,Error,Exception and RuntimeException. In later sections I will discuss each one of them.

Throwable Class

It is the mother class of all exception classes i.e. even if programmer has to create a user defined exception he has to inherit from Throwable class directly or indirectly. An exception that is not inherited from Throwable class directly or indirectly cannot be thrown (raised).

The Signature of Throwabe class is:

public class Throwable extends Object implements Serializable

The Throwable class inherits from Object class and it implements Serializable interface. Only objects that are instances of Throwable class (or one of its subclasses) are thrown by the Java Virtual Machine or can be thrown by the Java throw statement. Throwable class (exception) is compiler checked.

```
// Program 1
// Understanding Throwable class
   class Program {
       public static void main(String args[]) {
               throw new Throwable();
       }
   }
```

The Program gives compiler error. To overcome compiler error add "throws Throwable" as part main method definition.

```
// Program 2.
// Understanding Throwable class

class MyException {}

class Program {
public static void main(String args[]) {
        // throw new MyException();  // compiler error
    }
}
```

This program will give compiler error when code "throw new MyException" is uncommented. This is because only exception that is directly or indirectly derived from Throwable class can be raised.

Error Class

It is a child class of Throwable class. Error class represents all exceptions that are non-recoverable. A program can encounter a serious problem such as OutOfMemoryError,

StackoverflowError, VirtualMachineError etc. When a program encounter such situation the program crashes even if exception handling is done because these are non-recoverable exceptions. Let's understand this better with the help of a program. Error class is not compiler checked.

```
// Program 3
// Program to demonstrate Error class (StackoverflowError)

class Program {
    static void display(int i) {
        System.out.println("Display called :"+ i + "time");
        display(++i);
    }

    public static void main(String args[]) {
        display(0);
    }
}
```

In this program at some stage JVM will raise an un-recoverable StackoverflowError Exception. Error class (and subclasses) are also called as asynchronous exceptions.

Exception Class
It derives from Throwable class. Exception class (and subclasses) are recoverable exceptions. Normally Exception acts as mother class of user defined exceptions. Exception class is compiler checked i.e. if it is not handled programmer will get a complier error. The signature of Exception class is

   public class Exception extends Throwable

Let's understand Exception class better with help of a program.

```
// Program 4
// Description: Exception class behavior

class Program {
    public static void main(String args[]) {
        throw new Exception();
    }
}
```

This program will give compiler error because Exception class is compiler checked. To overcome compiler error either handle the exception or declare it with the main method.

RuntimeException Class
It is derived from Exception class. RuntimeException(and subclasses) are not compiler

checked. The signature of the Runtime class is

public class RuntimeException extends Exception

Generally RuntimeExceptions are exceptions that can be prevented programmatically. E.g. NullPointerException, ArithmeticException, ArrayIndexOutOfBoundException etc.
If programmer can check for null before calling any method, NullPointerException would never occur. Similarly ArrayIndexOutOfBoundException would never occur if you check the index first.

Let's understand RuntimeException better with the help of an example.

```
// Program 5
// RuntimeException(and child class) exceptions are not compiler checked
class Program {
 public static void main(String args[]) {
   throw new RuntimeException();
 }
}
```

When this program is compiled it won't give any error. When executed it would crash the program.

Summary
The Throwable class is the mother class of all classes in Java Exception hierarchy.Throwable and Exception classes are compiler checked. Error class represents non-recoverable exception and it is also non-recoverable. RuntimeException class is not compiler checked but is recoverable.

Chapter 5
Try and Catch Block

Topics
- ✓ **Life Cycle of an Unhandled Exception**
- ✓ **Try Block**
- ✓ **Catch Block**
- ✓ **Summary**

Life Cycle of an Unhandled Exception

When an exception is not handled then it will propagate in the call stack and ultimately it will be handled by JVM which will stop the program. Below I have illustrated the above steps in greater detail.

Step 1 -> After an exception object is created, it is handed over to the runtime system (thrown)

Step 2 -> The runtime system attempts to find a handler for the exception.

Step 3 -> If a handler is found, the exception is caught.

Step 4 -> If the handler is not found (the runtime backtracks all the way to the main () method), the exception stack trace is printed and the application aborts execution (Handled by JVM).

Let's understand the above process better with the help of an example.

```
// Program 1
// Description: Understanding life cycle of an unhandled exception

class Program {

  static void Method3() {
   System.out.println("Method3");
   int i=0;
   int j= 10/i;
  }
  static void Method2() {
   System.out.println("Method2");
```

```
        Method3();
    }

    static void Method1() {
    System.out.println("Method1");
    Method2();
    }

    public static void main(String arg[]) {
        Method1();
    }
  }
}
```

Output:

```
Method1
Method2
Method3
Exception in thread "main" java.lang.ArithmeticException: / by zero
        at Program.Method3(Prg.java:6)
        at Program.Method2(Prg.java:10)
        at Program.Method1(Prg.java:15)
        at Program.main(Prg.java:19)
```

As we can see that if an exception is not handled then program crashes and it display the call stack.

Try Block

It is a code block that identifies an area of code which has a probability of failure. Try block can be put inside

- Method
- Constructor
- Static block

Catch Block

It follows a try block. Catch block provide a mechanism for diagnosis and remedial steps to be taken for the occurred exception.

Following are the characteristics of catch block.

- It only exists if there is a try block.
- It immediately follows the try block.
- It is used to handle the exception.
- If the appropriate exception is not found the program crashes.

Syntax:

```
try {
......
} catch (ExceptionType name) {

} catch (ExceptionType name) {
............
}
```

```java
// Program 2
// Description: Handling Exception in constructor and Method

class Shape {

    void display() {
            System.out.println("Display of Shape Class");
    }
}
class Program {
  Shape obj;
 Program(String args[]) {

  int i=7;
  try {
   i= Integer.parseInt(args[0]); // NumberFormatException
  }catch(Exception e) {
     System.out.println("Exception happened :" + e);
  }
 }

  void CallMethod() {
     try {
            obj.display();// NullPointerException
     } catch(Exception e) {
            System.out.println("Exception Happened :" + e);
     }
  }


 public static void main(String args[]) {

    Program obj = new Program(args);
```

```
        obj.CallMethod();
    }
}
```

The above program when executed yields into
   a. NullPointerException when valid integer is passed at command line
   b. NumberFormatException when one of the argument is a character/string.

The above program demonstrate how to use try and catch blocks in method and constructor.

Let's learn how to use try and catch inside a static block.

```
// Program 3
// Description : Using try and catch inside a static block.

class Program {

static {
    int ar[] = new int[1];
        try {
                System.out.println("In Static Block:1");
                ar[0]=1;
                ar[1]=2; // ArrayIndexOutOfBoundsException
        }catch(Exception e) {
                System.out.println("Message is:"+ e);
        }
}

 static {

    int a=0,j=10;
        try {
                System.out.println("In Static Block:2");
                a=j/0; //ArithmeticException
        }catch(Exception e) {
                System.out.println("Message is:"+ e);
        }
}

public static void main(String args[]) {
        System.out.println("In main method");
    }
}
```

In the above program we can see how to use try and catch block in multiple static blocks.

Summary

Try block is a code block that identifies a code area that can possibly yield into an exception. Catch block is used for diagnosis of exception. Catch block follows try block. A try block can be put inside a method, constructor or static block.

Chapter 6
Exception Handling API

Topics
- ✓ **What is Call Stack?**
- ✓ **Using printStackTrace() Method**
- ✓ **Summary**

What is Call Stack?

It is a stack data structure that store information about the active functions of a program. If Exception is not handled call stack is printed. Knowing Call Stack information helps in identifying exceptions and troubleshooting them. Let's understand this with the help of an example.

```java
// Program 1
// Understanding call stack

class Program {
  static void Method3() {
   System.out.println("Method3");
   int i=0;
   int j= 10/i;
  }
  static void Method2() {
   System.out.println("Method2");
   Method3();
  }

  static void Method1() {
   System.out.println("Method1");
   Method2();
  }

  public static void main(String arg[]) {
    Method1();
  }
}
```

When control executes method3 it yields into a ArithmeticException which prints call stack info the screen.

Using printStackTrace() Method

printStackTrace() method is available from Throwable class.It gives details of call stack until the exception occurred. toString() method is overridden by Throwable class it return generic message for the exception occurred. Let's understand this better with help of an example.

```
//Program 2
//Description : Demonstration of printStackTrace() method

class Program {

  static void Method3() {
  try {
   System.out.println("Method3");
   int i=0;
   int j= 10/i;
  } catch(ArithmeticException e) {
        System.out.println("The Stack trace information is:");
        e.printStackTrace();
  }
  }
  static void Method2() {
   System.out.println("Method2");
   Method3();
  }

  static void Method1() {
   System.out.println("Method1");
   Method2();
  }

  public static void main(String arg[]) {
    Method1();
  }
}
```

Output:

```
Method1
Method2
Method3
The Stack trace information is:
java.lang.ArithmeticException: / by zero
        at Program.Method3(Prg2.java:7)
        at Program.Method2(Prg2.java:15)
        at Program.Method1(Prg2.java:20)
        at Program.main(Prg2.java:24)
```

As it can be inferred from output, printStackTrace() method display call stack info of the thread that encountered an exception.

Summary

Call stack is a stack data structure that store information about the active functions of a program. printStackTrace() method is defined in Throwable class, it prints call stack info of the exceptional thread.

Chapter 7
Multiple Catch

Topics
- ✓ **Multiple Catch Blocks**
- ✓ **Order of Catch Blocks**
- ✓ **Using Try Block Carefully**
- ✓ **Summary**

Multiple Catch Blocks

A 'try' block can have more than one catch blocks. At any given point of time only one exception can happen and the first best matching catch block is executed on the current thread.

Syntax

```
try {
.......//code
}catch (SomeException e) { .....}
  catch (SomeException e) {.....}
catch(SomeException e) { ...... }
```

Let's understand how to have multiple catch blocks for a given try block with the help of an example

```
// Program 1
// Description: Multiple catch Exception

class Program {
 public static void main(String args[]) {
   try {
        int i = Integer.parseInt(args[0]);
        int j = Integer.parseInt(args[1]);
        int k= i/j;
      }
      catch(ArrayIndexOutOfBoundsException e) {
        System.out.println(" ArrayIndexOutOfBoundsException Message is :"+e);
      }
      catch (ArithmeticException e) {
        System.out.println("The ArithmeticException message is:"+e);
      }
       catch(Exception e) {
```

```
        System.out.println("The Exception message is:"+e);
       }
     }
   }
```

Execute the above program by passing different types of arguments at command line.
At any given point in time only one catch block will be executed if there is an exception.

Order of Catch Blocks

When a programmer has multiple catch blocks for a try block then the exceptions have to be
handled in the reverse order(bottom-up) of the inheritance hierarchy. Let's understand this
with an example. Assume if a programmer has to catch Throwable, RuntimeException and
Exception (exceptions), since Throwable is the mother class of all exception classes it should
be caught at the last, Exception is the mother class of RuntimeException it would be caught
2nd last and RuntimeException class is at the bottom of the hierarchy it would appear in the
first catch block. If the above rule is not followed Java compiler gives an error. Let's
understand this better with the help of an example

```
//Program 2
// Understanding order of catch blocks
class Program {
  public static void main(String args[]) {
    try {
         int i = Integer.parseInt(args[0]);
         int j = Integer.parseInt(args[1]);
         int k= i/j;
       }
     catch(ArrayIndexOutOfBoundsException e) {
       System.out.println(" ArrayIndexOutOfBoundsException Message is :"+e);
     }
     catch (ArithmeticException e) {
       System.out.println("The ArithmeticException message is:"+e);
     }
     catch(Exception e) {
       System.out.println("The Exception message is:"+e);
     }
     catch(Throwable e) {
            System.out.println("The Throwable message is " + e)
     }
   }
}
```

As we can see the exceptions are caught in the reverse order of the inheritance hierarchy.
Since Throwable class is the mother class it is caught at the end.

Using Try Block Carefully

Try block can only be put inside a method, constructor or a static block. Try block cannot encapsulate a method, constructor, class or an interface. The below program which will yield into a compiler error.

```
// Program 3
// Description: Illegal try block
// Compiler error

class Program {
    Program() {
        System.out.println("Program constructor");
    }
    try {   // cannot encapsulate a method
public static void main(String args[]) {

        int i = Integer.parseInt(args[0]);
        int j = Integer.parseInt(args[1]);
        int k= i/j;
    }
    catch (Exception e) {
        System.out.println("The message is " + e)
    }
}
```

Summary
A try block can have multiple catch blocks, these catch blocks have placed in the reverse order of the inheritance hierarchy. Try block cannot encapsulate class, constructor, method or an interface.

Chapter 8
Multiple Exceptions

Topics
- ✓ **Catching Multiple Exception in a Single Catch**
- ✓ **Summary**

Catching Multiple Exception in a Single Catch

This feature was added to Java in version 7. Using this capability programmer can specify multiple exception in a single catch block.

Syntax:

```
try {
              ...
} catch( IOException | SQLException ex ) {
      ...
}
```

The catch block is executed when any of the exception occur. The exception object is instantiated only once i.e. after the last exception in the sequence. It is important to note that mother and child class exception cannot be handled in the same catch. The below code will give error.

Syntax:

```
try {
              ...
} catch( Throwable | Exception ex ) {
      ...
}
```

```
// Program 1
// Description: Using multiple exceptions in a single catch

class Program {
 public static void main(String args[]) {
   try {
        int i = Integer.parseInt(args[0]);
        int j = Integer.parseInt(args[1]);
        int k= i/j;
```

```
        } catch(ArrayIndexOutOfBoundsException | ArithmeticException  e) {
                // Object is created only once
            System.out.println("The message is:"+e);
        }
        // Requires another program - Alternatives in subclassing
        catch(ArrayIndexOutOfBoundsException | ArithmeticException | Exception  e) {
            System.out.println("The message is:"+e);
        }

        catch(Throwable e) {
                System.out.println("The Throwable message is " + e);
        }
    }
}
```

The above will yield into a compiler error.

Output:

```
Prg.java:13: error: Alternatives in a multi-catch statement cannot be related by subclassing
        catch(ArrayIndexOutOfBoundsException | ArithmeticException | Exception  e) {
                                                                     ^
   Alternative ArrayIndexOutOfBoundsException is a subclass of alternative Exception
```

If the second catch block is removed from the above program it will compile correctly. Let's see the changed program.

```
// Program 2
// Description: Demo of multiple exceptions in a single catch

class Program {
public static void main(String args[]) {
  try {
        int i = Integer.parseInt(args[0]);
        int j = Integer.parseInt(args[1]);
        int k= i/j;
    } catch(ArrayIndexOutOfBoundsException | ArithmeticException  e) {
            // Object is created only once
        System.out.println("The message is:"+e);
    }

    catch(Throwable e) {
            System.out.println("The Throwable message is " + e);
    }
}
```

}

This program will yield into an exception (ArrayIndexOutOfBoundsException) if command line argument in not passed.

Output:
```
The message is:java.lang.ArrayIndexOutOfBoundsException: 0
```

Summary

From Java 7 onwards programmer can handle multiple exceptions in a single catch.

Chapter 9
Finally Block

Topics
- ✓ **What is 'Finally' Block?**
- ✓ **Using 'Finally' Block.**
- ✓ **Advanced Try Block.**
- ✓ **Summary**

What is 'Finally' Block?

It is placed after the catch block (only when the catch block exists), it can also be placed after try block is there is no catch block. The finally block is executed if there is an exception and also when there is no exception. This make finally block confusing to use. A very important attribute of finally block is that it is guaranteed to be executed except when the program is abruptly terminated.

Using Finally Block

For a given try block there can only be one finally block but there can be many catch blocks. It is principally used for executing housekeeping code. Housekeeping code performs initialization and closing of resources. Finally block is also used for performing logging of exceptions. Program below explain about the execution behavior of finally block.

```
// Program 1
// Description: Finally block is executed irrespective of exception occurrence.


class Program {
 public static void main(String args[]) {
        boolean isException = false;
    try {
          int i = Integer.parseInt(args[0]);
          int j = Integer.parseInt(args[1]);
          int k= i/j;
        } catch(ArrayIndexOutOfBoundsException e) {
          System.out.println(" ArrayIndexOutOfBoundsException Message is :"+e);
          isException= true;
        }catch (ArithmeticException e) {
          System.out.println("The ArithmeticException message is:"+e);
          isException= true;
```

```
      }
      catch(Exception e) {
        System.out.println("The Exception message is:"+e);
        isException= true;
      }


      finally {
            if(isException)
            System.out.println("The finally block is executed when there is
            exception");
            else
            System.out.println("The finally block is also executed when there is no
            exception");
      }
   }
}
```

The output of the program
   a. When there is an exception (Pass 10 0 at command line).

```
The ArithmeticException message is:java.lang.ArithmeticException: / by zero
The finally block is executed when there is exception
```

as it can seen that finally block is executed when there is exception in the program.

b. When there is no exception

```
The finally block is also executed when there is no exception
```

The finally block is exeuted when there is no exception in the program.


```
//Program 2
//Description : There can only be one finally block per try block.
// finally block behaviour

class Program {
 public static void main(String args[]) {
      boolean isException = false;
   try {
        int i = Integer.parseInt(args[0]);
        int j = Integer.parseInt(args[1]);
        int k= i/j;
      } catch(ArrayIndexOutOfBoundsException e) {
        System.out.println(" ArrayIndexOutOfBoundsException Message is :"+e);
```

30

```
        isException= true;
    }catch (ArithmeticException e) {
       System.out.println("The ArithmeticException message is:"+e);
       isException= true;
    }
    catch(Exception e) {
       System.out.println("The Exception message is:"+e);
       isException= true;
    }


    finally {
          if(isException)
                System.out.println("The finally block is executed when there is
exception");
          else
                System.out.println("The finally block is also executed when there
is no exception");
    }

    finally { //error

    }
  }
}
```

Output : The above program will give compiler error (finally without try).

Advanced Try Block

It is not mandatory to have both catch and finally block together for the a given try block. Try block can have either catch or finally block. If both catch and finally blocks are present for a try block then catch block comes first then followed by finally block.

If the try block only has finally block then if an exception occurs the program will crash after executing the finally block. Let's understand this better with help of a program.


```
// Program 3
// Description : try block with only finally block

class Program {
 public static void main(String args[]) {
       boolean isException = false;
   try {
         int i = Integer.parseInt(args[0]);
```

```
        int j = Integer.parseInt(args[1]);
         int k= i/j;
     }
      finally {
                    System.out.println("The finally block is executed");
      }


   }
   }
```

If an exception occur in the above program it will crash. To perform diagnosis catch block is needed.

Summary
 Finally block is used for executing housekeeping code. It is executed irrespective of exception occurrence. Optionally Try block can just have either catch or finally blocks.

Chapter 10
Finally block & Return keyword

Topics
- ✓ **Using Finally Block and Return keyword.**
- ✓ **Summary.**

Using Finally Block and Return Keyword

Finally block will be executed even if return keyword instruction is executed from within the try block. Finally block will also be executed even if return keyword instruction is executed from a catch block. It won't be executed if control encounter System.exit() function anywhere.

```
// Program 1
// Description: Finally block is executed even when control encounter return keyword

class Program {
 public static void main(String args[]) {
        boolean isException = false;
   try {
        int i = Integer.parseInt(args[0]);
        int j = Integer.parseInt(args[1]);

        int k= i/j;
        return;
    } catch(ArrayIndexOutOfBoundsException e) {
      System.out.println(" ArrayIndexOutOfBoundsException Message is :"+e);
      isException= true;
      return;
    }catch (ArithmeticException e) {
      System.out.println("The ArithmeticException message is:"+e);
      isException= true;
      return;
    }
    catch(Exception e) {
      System.out.println("The Exception message is:"+e);
      isException= true;
      return;
    }

        finally {
```

```
            if(!isException)
                    System.out.println("The finally block is executed when there is
return from method");
                else
                    System.out.println("The finally block is also executed when there
return from catch");
        }
    }
}
```

Output: The finally block is executed

```
// Program 2
//Description: The finally block is not executed when control encounter System.exit()
function.

class Program {
 public static void main(String args[]) {
        boolean isException = false;
   try {
        int i = Integer.parseInt(args[0]);
        int j = Integer.parseInt(args[1]);
        System.exit(0);
        int k= i/j;
     } catch(ArrayIndexOutOfBoundsException e) {
       System.out.println(" ArrayIndexOutOfBoundsException Message is :"+e);
       isException= true;
       return;
     }catch (ArithmeticException e) {
       System.out.println("The ArithmeticException message is:"+e);
       isException= true;
       return;
     }
     catch(Exception e) {
       System.out.println("The Exception message is:"+e);
       isException= true;
       return;
     }


        finally { // finally block is not executed when the program aborts.
            if(!isException)
                System.out.println("The finally block is executed when there is return
```

34

```
              from method");
                         else
                         System.out.println("The finally block is also executed when there return
         from catch");
                    }
            }
     }
```

Output: The finally block is not executed.

Summary
The finally block is guaranteed to be executed even if return keyword is encountered. The finally block will not be executed if System.exit() function is executed.

Chapter 11
Checked and Unchecked Exception

Topics
- ✓ **Throws Keyword**
- ✓ **Checked Exception**
- ✓ **Unchecked Exception**

Throws Keyword

It is used for declaring an exception for a method. It help in pre-empting an exception for a given method. A method can 'throws' multiple exception. Exception that is 'throws' from a method has to be handled else compiler will prompt an error.

Syntax:

void PerformIO() throws IOException { .... }

Let's understand "throws" keyword with the help of an example.

```
//Program 1
//Description: Understanding throws keyword usage

import java.io.*;
class Program {
        static void AcceptData() throws IOException {
                int i = System.in.read();
        }
        public static void main(String args[]) throws Throwable {
                throw new Throwable();
        }
}
```

In the program above is it mandatory to handle IOException for AcceptData method. One way to handle it would be to declare the exception using throws. The same would apply for main method.

Checked Exception

These are those exceptions that are identified by the compiler. All classes that inherit from Throwable or Exception class are checked exceptions. The compiler will flag an error if a checked exception is not handled. Checked exception have to be handled. It is an excellent way to enhance reliability of a program. Let's understand checked exception better with an example.

```
//Program 2
// Understanding checked exception

import java.io.*;
class Program {
        static void AcceptData() {
                int i = System.in.read();
        }
        public static void main(String args[]) {
                throw new Throwable();
        }
}
```

Output: A checked exception has to be handled.

```
Prg.java:7: error: unreported exception IOException; must be caught or declared to be thrown
             int i = System.in.read();
                                    ^
Prg.java:10: error: unreported exception Throwable; must be caught or declared to be thrown
             throw new Throwable();
                  ^
2 errors
```

A checked exception can be handled in two ways
   a. Try... Catch blocks
   b. Throws keyword

Unchecked Exception
It is not identified by the compiler. It is also called as runtime exception. All classes that inherit from RuntimeException class are Unchecked. Some examples of unchecked exception are NullPointerException, ArithmeticException and ClassCastException.

```
//Program 3
// Description: Understanding unchecked exceptions
import java.io.*;
class Program {
        public static void main(String args[]) {
                throw new RuntimeException(); // Can be avoided by performing a check.

        }
}
```
In above program compiler will not report any error hence it is unchecked exception.

Summary
Checked exceptions are captured by compiler. Unchecked exceptions are identified at runtime. 'throws' keyword is used to declare exception as part of method definition.

Chapter 12
Nested Exception

Topics
- ✓ **Implementing Nested Exception**
- ✓ **Life Cycle of Nested Exception Handling**
- ✓ **Summary**

Implementing Nested Exception

When try blocks are nested it is called as nesting of exception i.e. When a try block is within another try block it is called as nesting of exception. Java supports nesting of exception up to any depth. Let's understand this with the help of an example.

```java
// Program 1
// Description: Nesting of Exception

class Program {
    static void Sum(String ar[]) {
        try {
            int i = Integer.parseInt(ar[0]);
            int j = Integer.parseInt(ar[1]);
            int sum = i+j;
            System.out.println("The sum is :"+sum);
        }catch (NumberFormatException e) {
            System.out.println("Numberformatexception message is"+e);
        }
    }
    public static void main(String args[]) {
        try
        {
            Sum(args);
        }catch(ArrayIndexOutOfBoundsException e) {
            System.out.println("ArrayIndexOutOfBoundsException message is:"+ e);
        }
    }
}
```

Output:
If the user doesn't pass any argument then program is going to fail in the Sum method during type conversion. The exception ArrayIndexOutOfBoundsException that is generated will not be caught by the inner catch but will be caught by the outer catch.

Life Cycle of Nested Exception Handling

The working of nested exception handling can be identified in three steps i.e.

1. When an exception occur within a nested try the inner most try's 'catch+finally' get an opportunity to handle first.

2. If the inner try cannot handle the exception the outer try's catch/finally gets an opportunity.

3. If the outer try cannot handle then program crashes.

4. If an exception is handled in inner catch then it won't bubble to the outer try. An exception is caught only once even in nested exceptions.

Behavior:
   a. Finally block of all try blocks will be executed irrespective of exception occurrence.

   b. If an exception is caught in inner try it won't bubble and finally block if it is available it will be executed (Inner and Outer blocks).

Let's understand the handling of nested exception with the help of a program.

```java
// Program 2
// Description: Life Cycle of Nested Exception Handling

class Program {
    static void Sum(String ar[]) {
        try {
            int i = Integer.parseInt(ar[0]);
            int j = Integer.parseInt(ar[1]);
            int Sum = i+j;
            System.out.println("The result is :"+Sum);
        }catch (NumberFormatException e) {
            System.out.println("Numberformatexception message is"+e);
        }
        finally {
            System.out.println("Finally of inner try");
        }
    }
```

```java
public static void main(String args[]) {
    try
    {
        Sum(args);
    }catch(ArrayIndexOutOfBoundsException e) {
        System.out.println("ArrayIndexOutOfBoundsException message is
        :"+ e);
    }
    finally {
        System.out.println("Finally of outer try");
    }
}
}
```

Output 1: When user passes one of the argument to be string. Inner exception is handled and both the finally blocks are executed

```
Numberformatexception message isjava.lang.NumberFormatException: For input string: "b"
Finally of inner try
Finally of outer try
```

Output 2: When the user passes both arguments as integers. There are no exceptions but both finally blocks are executed.

```
The result is :20
Finally of inner try
Finally of outer try
```

Output 3: When user does not pass any argument. The outer catch is executed and both the finally blocks are executed.

```
Finally of inner try
ArrayIndexOutOfBoundsException message is :java.lang.ArrayIndexOutOfBoundsException: 1
Finally of outer try
```

Summary
Java allows nesting of exception. Inner most try gets first chance to handle the exception. If all try do not handle the exception then JVM handles hence program crashes.

Chapter 13
'Throw' Keyword

Topics
- ✓ **Using 'throw' Keyword**
- ✓ **Summary**

Using 'throw' Keyword
The 'throw' keyword is used for raising an exception. Only classes that inherit from Throwable class can be raised (thrown).

Syntax:
Throw object   or throw new "classname"
e.g.   throw myobj   or   throw new Exception()

Let's us understand usage of throw keyword with help of an example.

```
// Program 1
// Description: Understanding usage of throw keyword

class Test {}
class Program {
public static void main(String args[]) throws Exception{
       throw new IOException();
       throw new Test(); // Compiler error

}
}
```

Some observation on the above program:
  a. Only Object derived from Throwable can be thrown.
  b. If a checked exception is thrown then it has to handled.

Summary
Throw keyword is used to raise exception.

Chapter 14
Exception Chaining

Topics
- ✓ **What is Exception Chaining?**
- ✓ **Implementing Exception Chaining**
- ✓ **Summary**

What is Exception Chaining?
When the first exception raises the second exception, second has information about the first hence first and second exceptions are in a chain. It is mainly used to enhance diagnosis when performing nested exception handling. This way programmer can relate one exception to the next hence creating a chain.

Implementing Exception Chaining
The capability for Exception chaining is provided by Throwable class. The Throwable class has constructors and methods to help in creating exception chain.

Let's look at the API provided by Throwable class
- a. Constructors
    - i. Throwable(String, Throwable)
    - ii. Throwable(Throwable)
- b. Methods
    - i. Throwable getCause()
    - ii. Throwable initCause(Throwable)

The 'Throwable' argument to constructors and initCause() method is the exception that caused the current exception. Exceptions can be chained upto any depth.

Let's understand how exception chaining is implemented with the help of constructors.

```java
// Program 1
// Description: Creating exception chain

class NegativeNumberException extends ArithmeticException {
        public NegativeNumberException(String str) {
                super(str);
        }
}
```

```java
class ZeroNumberException extends ArithmeticException {
        public ZeroNumberException(String str) {
                super(str);
        }
}

class Program {

        static int Divide (int i, int j)throws Throwable {
                try {
                        if ( i < 0 || j < 0)
                                throw new NegativeNumberException("One of the numbers
is negative");
                        else if ( j==0)
                                throw new ZeroNumberException("Divisor is zero");
                        int res = i/j;
                        return res;
                } catch (ArithmeticException e ) {
                                throw new Throwable (e);
                }
        }

        public static void main(String args[]) {
                try {
                int i = Integer.parseInt(args[0]);
                int j = Integer.parseInt(args[1]);
                Divide(i,j);
                } catch(Throwable e) {
                        System.out.println("The Message is "+ e);
                }

        }
}
```

In the above program I have created 2 user defined exceptions. To create exception chain pass a negative number at command line that would create an exception chain. The chain created in the above program has 2 exceptions in chain i.e. NegativeNumberException ->Throwable.

Let's understand how to use initCause() and getCause() methods.

```java
//Program 2
//Description: Using initCause and getCause methods
import java.io.*;
```

```java
class NegativeNumberException extends ArithmeticException {
    public NegativeNumberException(String str) {
        super(str);
    }
}

class ZeroNumberException extends ArithmeticException {
    public ZeroNumberException(String str) {
        super(str);
    }
}

class Program {
    static void Divide (int i, int j)throws Exception {
        try {
            if ( i < 0 || j < 0) {
                NegativeNumberException obj =  new
                NegativeNumberException("One of the numbers is
                negative");
                throw obj;
            }
            else if ( j==0) {
                ZeroNumberException obj2 = new
                ZeroNumberException("Divisor is zero");
                throw obj2;
            }
            int res = i/j;
            System.out.println(res);
        } catch (ArithmeticException e ) {
            try {
                FileInputStream fin = new
                FileInputStream("MyFile.txt");
            }catch(IOException e2) {
                e2.initCause(e);
                throw e2;
            }
        }
    }

    public static void main(String args[]) {
        try {
            int i = Integer.parseInt(args[0]);
            int j = Integer.parseInt(args[1]);
            Divide(i,j);
        } catch(Exception e) {
            System.out.println("The Message is "+ e.getCause());
```

```
System.out.println("\n\n StackTrace info");
e.printStackTrace();
System.out.println("\n\n StackTrace info : inner exception");
e.getCause().printStackTrace();

            }
        }
    }
```

The above program can be broken up into three steps when user passes negative numbers at command line.

a. NegativeNumberException is thrown from divide method, which is caught in divide method.
b. The catch of the divide method raises FileInputStream exception which identifies NegativeNumberException as the cause.
c. The catch of the main method captures FileInputStream Exception and display stack trace info. The details of inner exception is extracted using getCause() method.

The chain that is created is:
NegativeNumberException(Inner) -> FileInputStream (Outer)

Output:
```
The Message is NegativeNumberException: One of the numbers is negative


 StackTrace info
java.io.FileNotFoundException: MyFile.txt (The system cannot find the file specified)
        at java.io.FileInputStream.open(Native Method)
        at java.io.FileInputStream.<init>(Unknown Source)
        at java.io.FileInputStream.<init>(Unknown Source)
        at Program.Divide(Prg2.java:34)
        at Program.main(Prg2.java:46)
Caused by: NegativeNumberException: One of the numbers is negative
        at Program.Divide(Prg2.java:23)
        ... 1 more


 StackTrace info : inner exception
NegativeNumberException: One of the numbers is negative
        at Program.Divide(Prg2.java:23)
        at Program.main(Prg2.java:46)
```

Summary
Exception chaining is accomplished using Throwable class constructor, initCause() and getCause() methods. Exception chaining help in easy diagnosis of nested exceptions.

Chapter 15
Try with Resource

Topics
- ✓ **What is Try with Resource?**
- ✓ **Implementing Try with Resource**
- ✓ **Summary**

What is Try with Resource?
This feature was introduced in Java 7. Using this feature programmer can perform automatic resource management. A resource is an object that is used in program and must be closed after the program is finished. The try-with-resources statement ensures that each resource is closed at the end of the statement. Programmer need not have to explicitly close the resources.

Syntax:
```
try(resource-specification)
{
        //use the resource
} catch(e){
    ...
}
```
This try statement contains a parenthesis in which one or more resources is declared.

Implementing Try with Resource
Any object that implements java.lang.AutoCloseable or java.io.Closeable, can be passed as a parameter to try statement. Autocloseable/Closeable interface has only close method. It is called automatically when the try block finishes. Multiple resources can be instantiated inside try i.e they are separated by a semi-colon. The resources are closed in the reverse order of creation.

Let's see how to use try with resource.

```
// Program 1
// Description: Without using Try with resource
import java.io.*;

class Shape implements Closeable {
        public void close() {
                System.out.println("Shape object close is closed");
        }
}
```

```
class Program {
        public static void main(String args[]){
                try {
                        Shape obj = new Shape();
                }catch(Exception e) {
                        System.out.println("Exception happened" + e);
                }
        }
}
```

In the above program the object of shape does not call close method automatically but it has to be called manually.

```
//Program 2
//Description: Using try with resource

import java.io.*;

class Shape implements Closeable {
        public void close() {
                System.out.println("Shape object close is closed");
        }
        public void display() {
                System.out.println("Display of shape");
        }
}
class Program {
        public static void main(String args[]){
                try(Shape obj = new Shape()) {
                        obj.display();
                }catch(Exception e) {
                        System.out.println("Exception happened" + e);
                }
        }
}
```

In this program the object of shape is called automatically. As it can be seen in the output.

Output:

```
Display of shape
Shape object close is closed
```

```java
// Program 3
// Description: Creating multiple objects in try with resource statement.

import java.io.*;

class Shape implements Closeable {
    public void close() {
        System.out.println("Shape object is closed");
    }
    public void display() {
        System.out.println("Display of shape");
    }
}
class Circle  extends Shape {

}

class Ellipse extends Circle {
    public void close() {
        System.out.println("Ellipse object is closed");
    }
    public void show() {
        System.out.println("Show of ellipse");
    }
}

class Program {
    public static void main(String args[]){
        try(Shape obj = new Shape(); Circle obj2 = new Circle();Ellipse obj3 =
new Ellipse()) {
            obj.display();
            obj2.display();
            obj3.show();
        }catch(Exception e) {
            System.out.println("Exception happened" + e);
        }
    }
}
```

The above program demonstrate that objects are closed in the reverse order of creation. The circle class does not implement close() method hence close() method of Shape class is called.

Output:

```
Display of shape
Display of shape
Show of ellipse
Ellipse object is closed
Shape object is closed
Shape object is closed
```

Summary

It is a way to perform automatic resource management. The object has to implement AutoCloseable or Closeable interface. More than one object can be created in the 'try' block.

Chapter 16
Exception Handling and Method Overriding

Topics
- ✓ **Rules for Exception Handling for Overridden methods.**
- ✓ **Summary**

Rules for Exception Handling for Overridden methods.

Special care has to be taken when performing exception handling for overridden methods. There are certain conditions that has to be satisfied or else compiler will report an error. Let's understand the rules that have to be followed.

Rule 1: If mother class method does not 'throws' any exception then

    a. The child class overridden method cannot 'throws' checked exception.
    b. The child class overridden method can 'throws' unchecked exception.

Let's verify rule1 with help of an example

```java
// Program 1
// Description: Verifying Rule 1

import java.io.*;

class Shape {
 void draw () {
       System.out.println ("Drawing Shape");
 }

 void draw3d() {
       System.out.println("Drawing 3D Shape");
 }
}

class Circle extends Shape{
       void draw() throws RuntimeException {
             System.out.println("Drawing Circle");
       }

       void draw3d() throws IOException {
             System.out.println("Drawing 3D Circle");
```

```
            }
    }

    class Program {
        public static void main(String args[]) {
            Circle obj = new Circle();
            obj.draw();
        }
    }
```

In the above program draw() method of Shape class does not "throws" any exception and it is overridden by draw() method of Circle class. The draw() method of Circle class "throws" RuntimeException which is an unchecked exception hence compiler does not report any error. Whereas draw3d() method when overridden "throws" IOException which is a checked exception hence it is reported by the compiler.

Output:
```
Prg.java:18: error: draw3d() in Circle cannot override draw3d() in Shape
        void draw3d() throws IOException {
             ^
  overridden method does not throw IOException
1 error
```

Rule 2: If the mother class method "throws" an exception then

    a. Child class method need not 'throws' any exception.
    b. The Child class can 'throws' the same exception or child class of that exception.

Let's verify the above rule with help of a program.

```
//Program 2
//Description: Verifying Rule 2

import java.io.*;

class Shape {
  void draw () throws Exception {
        System.out.println ("Drawing shape");
  }
  void draw3d() throws Exception {
        System.out.println("Drawing 3D shape");
  }
  void show() throws Exception {
        System.out.println("This is show method");
  }
}
```

```
class Circle extends Shape{
        void draw() throws Throwable {
                System.out.println("Drawing Circle");
        }
        void draw3d() {
                System.out.println("Drawing 3D circle");
        }

        void show() throws IOException {
                System.out.println("Show method of circle");
        }
}
class Program {
        public static void main(String args[]) throws Exception{
                Circle obj = new Circle();
                obj.draw();
        }
}
```

In the above program
   a. Shape class draw() method "throws" Exception class and child class Circle draw()
      method "throws" Throwable class which will yield into a compiler error. This is
      because the Child class can "throws" the same exception or child class of that
      exception.
   b. Shape class draw3d() method "throws" Exception class and child class Circle
      draw3d() method does not "throws" any exception hence compiler does not report
      any exception.
   c. Shape class show() method "throws" Exception class and child class Circle show()
      method "throws" IOException class which will not yield into any compiler error. This
      because IOException class is a child class of Exception class.

Output:

```
Prg2.java:16: error: draw() in Circle cannot override draw() in Shape
        void draw() throws Throwable {
             ^
  overridden method does not throw Throwable
1 error
```

Summary

Rules apply for overridden method when using 'throws' keyword. If the super class method 'throws' an exception then child class can 'throws' the same exception or child class of that exception. If super class method does not 'throws' any exception then the child class overridden method can 'throws' unchecked exception.

Chapter 17
User Defined Exception

Topics
- ✓ **Creating User Defined Exception**
- ✓ **Summary**

Creating User Defined Exception

User defined exception represent a business rule violation. In a typical software application maximum exceptions that are raised and handled are user defined. Some of the examples of user defined exception in an ATM application could be.

- a. ATMException
- b. OutOfFundsException
- c. AuthenticationFailure

A User defined exception is created by inheriting from Throwable or Exception class, it is better to inherit from Exception class because it offer enhanced functionality.
A User defined exception is initialized by using mother class constructor. A UDE(user defined exception) can override toString() method to provide custom message.

Let's understand UDE with help of examples

```
//Program 1
//Description: Creating user define exception


        class PositiveNumberException extends Exception {
                int n;
                PositiveNumberException(String msg,int num) {
                        super(msg);
                        n = num;
                }
                public String toString () {
                        return "The number "+n + " is not positive";
                }
        }

        class Program {
                public static void main(String args[]) {
                        try {
```

```
                    int i = Integer.parseInt(args[0]);
            if ( i <0 )
             throw new PositiveNumberException("The number is not positive",i);
            }catch(PositiveNumberException e) {
                    System.out.println(e.toString());
            }
        }
    }
```

When the user passes a negative number at command line UDE PositiveNumberException is raised. The UDE PositiveNumberException is derived from Exception class.

Output:

```
The number -10 is not positive
```

```
    // Program 2
    // Description: Using UDE with "throws" keyword

    class PositiveNumberException extends Exception {
        int n;
        PositiveNumberException(String msg,int num) {
            super(msg);
            n = num;
        }
        public String toString () {
         return " Throws keyword with UDE ->The number "+n + " is not positive";
        }
    }

    class Program {
        static void check(String args[]) throws PositiveNumberException {
            int i = Integer.parseInt(args[0]);
            if ( i <0 )
             throw new PositiveNumberException("The number is not positive",i);
        }
        public static void main(String args[]) {
            try {
                    check(args);
            }catch(PositiveNumberException e) {
                    System.out.println(e.toString());
            }
        }
    }
```

In above program check method throws PositiveNumberException.

Output:

```
Throws keyword with UDE -> The number -19 is not positive
```

Summary

UDE is a business rule violation. UDE is created by inheriting from Exception or Throwable class. UDE can be used with "throws" keyword.